In a Cast

Level 4 – Blue

Helpful Hints for Reading at Home

The graphemes (written letters) and phonemes (units of sound) used throughout this series are aligned with Letters and Sounds. This offers a consistent approach to learning, whether reading at home or in the classroom.

HERE IS A LIST OF PHONEMES FOR THIS PHASE OF LEARNING. AN EXAMPLE OF THE PRONUNCIATION CAN BE FOUND IN BRACKETS.

Phase 3			
j (jug)	v (van)	w (wet)	x (fox)
y (yellow)	z (zoo)	zz (buzz)	qu (quick)
ch (chip)	sh (shop)	th (thin/then)	ng (ring)
ai (rain)	ee (feet)	igh (night)	oa (boat)
oo (boot/look)	ar (farm)	or (for)	ur (hurt)
ow (cow)	oi (coin)	ear (dear)	air (fair)
ure (sure)	er (corner)		

HERE ARE SOME WORDS WHICH YOUR CHILD MAY FIND TRICKY.

Phase 3 Tricky Words			
he	you	she	they
we	all	me	are
be	my	was	her

Phase 4 Tricky Words			
said	were	have	there
like	little	so	one
do	when	some	out
come	what		

TOP TIPS FOR HELPING YOUR CHILD TO READ:

- Allow children time to break down unfamiliar words into units of sound and then encourage children to string these sounds together to create the word.

- Encourage your child to point out any focus phonics when they are used.

- Read through the book more than once to grow confidence.

- Ask simple questions about the text to assess understanding.

- Encourage children to use illustrations as prompts.

This book focuses on /ow/ and /ure/ and is a Blue level 4 book band.

Can you sort all the words on this page into two groups?

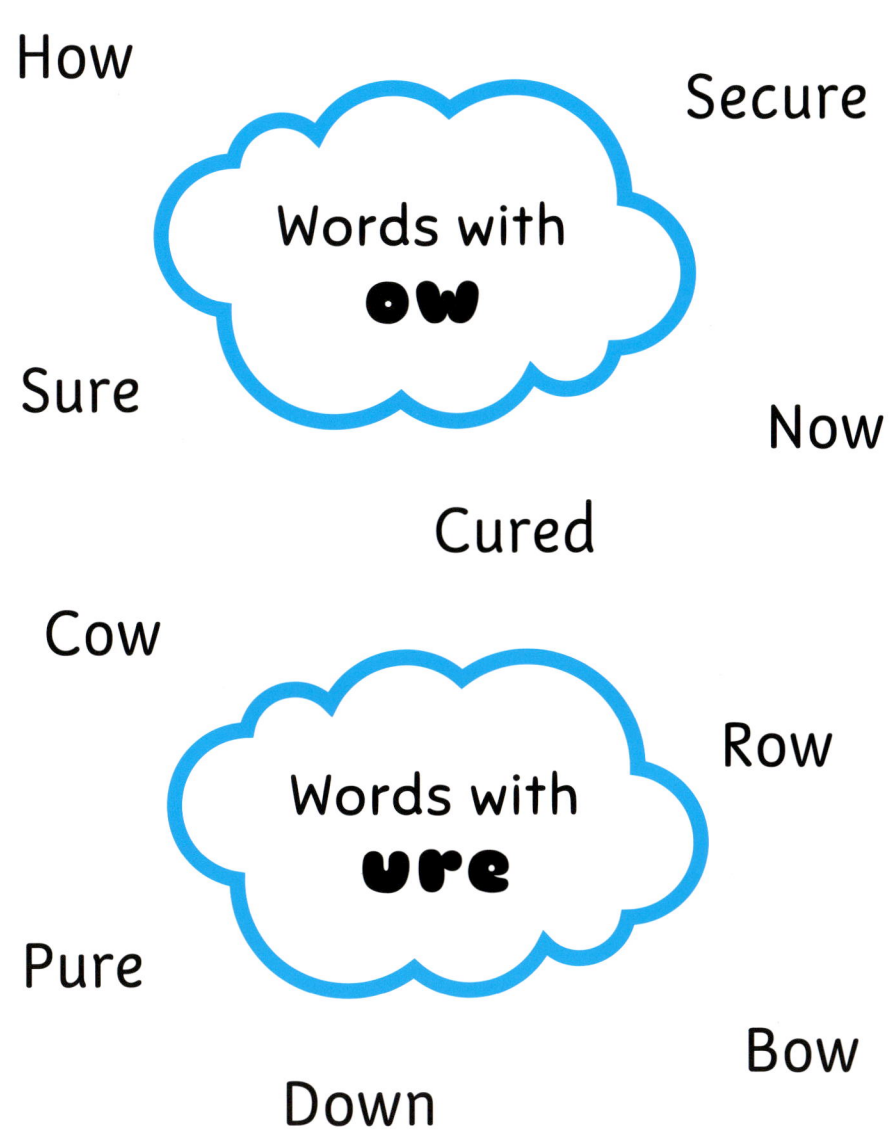

How

Secure

Sure

Now

Cured

Cow

Row

Pure

Bow

Down

Her leg is in pain. How did she injure it? It was when she fell off.

Can they cure her? They need to look at the leg to see if they can help.

If they are not sure what the problem is, they can get a picture.

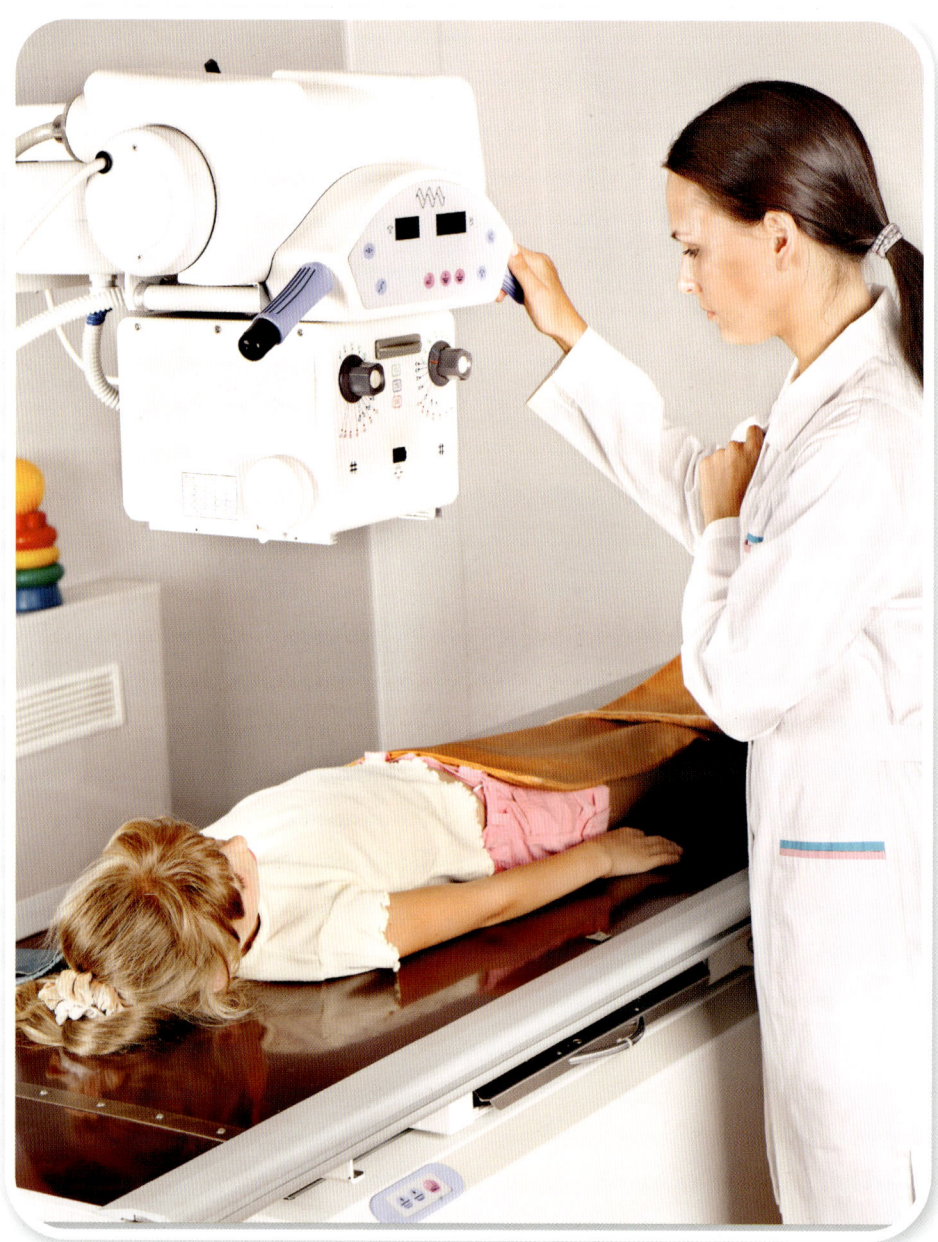

Will she need a gown? No, she can dress how she likes.

Gown

Now they are sure. There is a problem with her leg. It is a fracture.

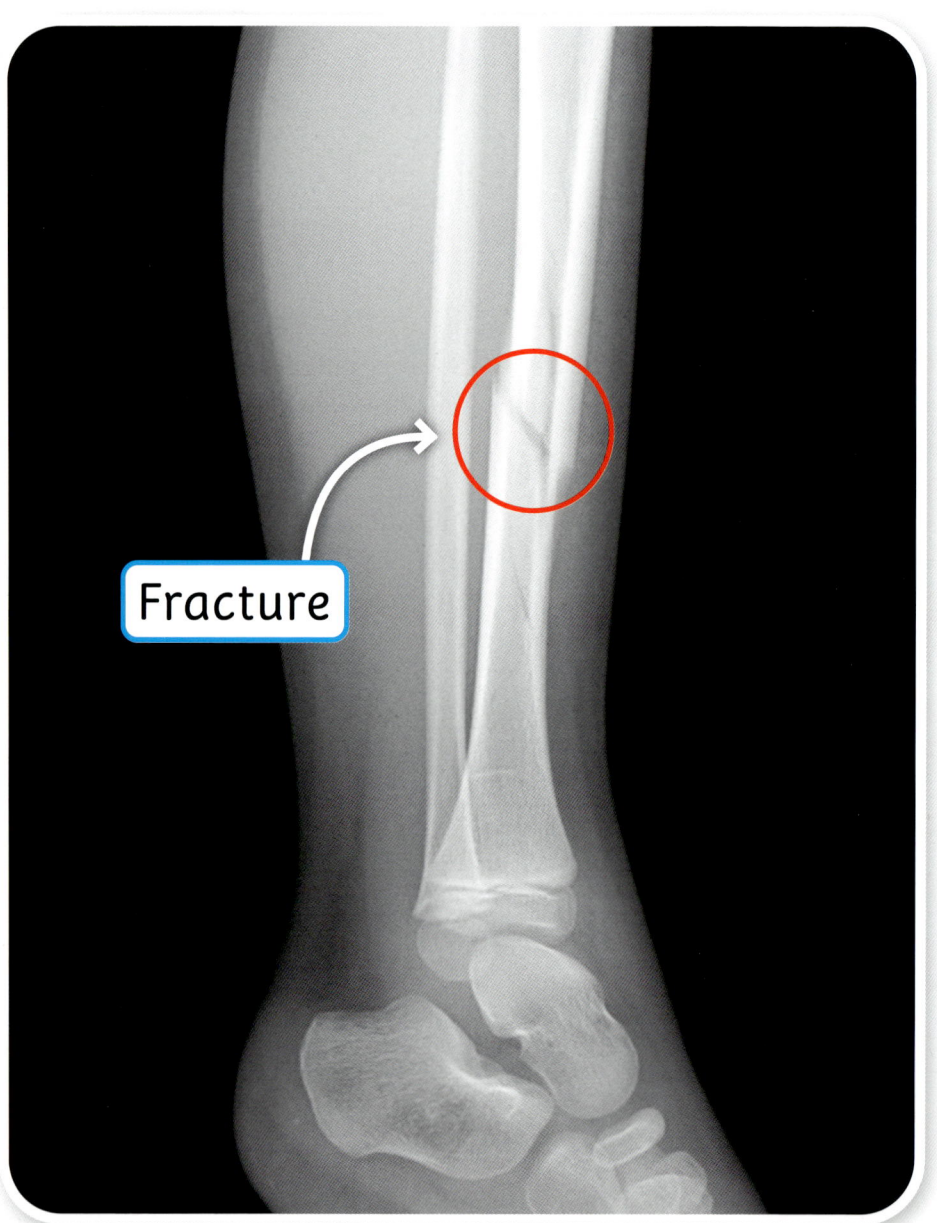

She will need to get a cast on her leg.

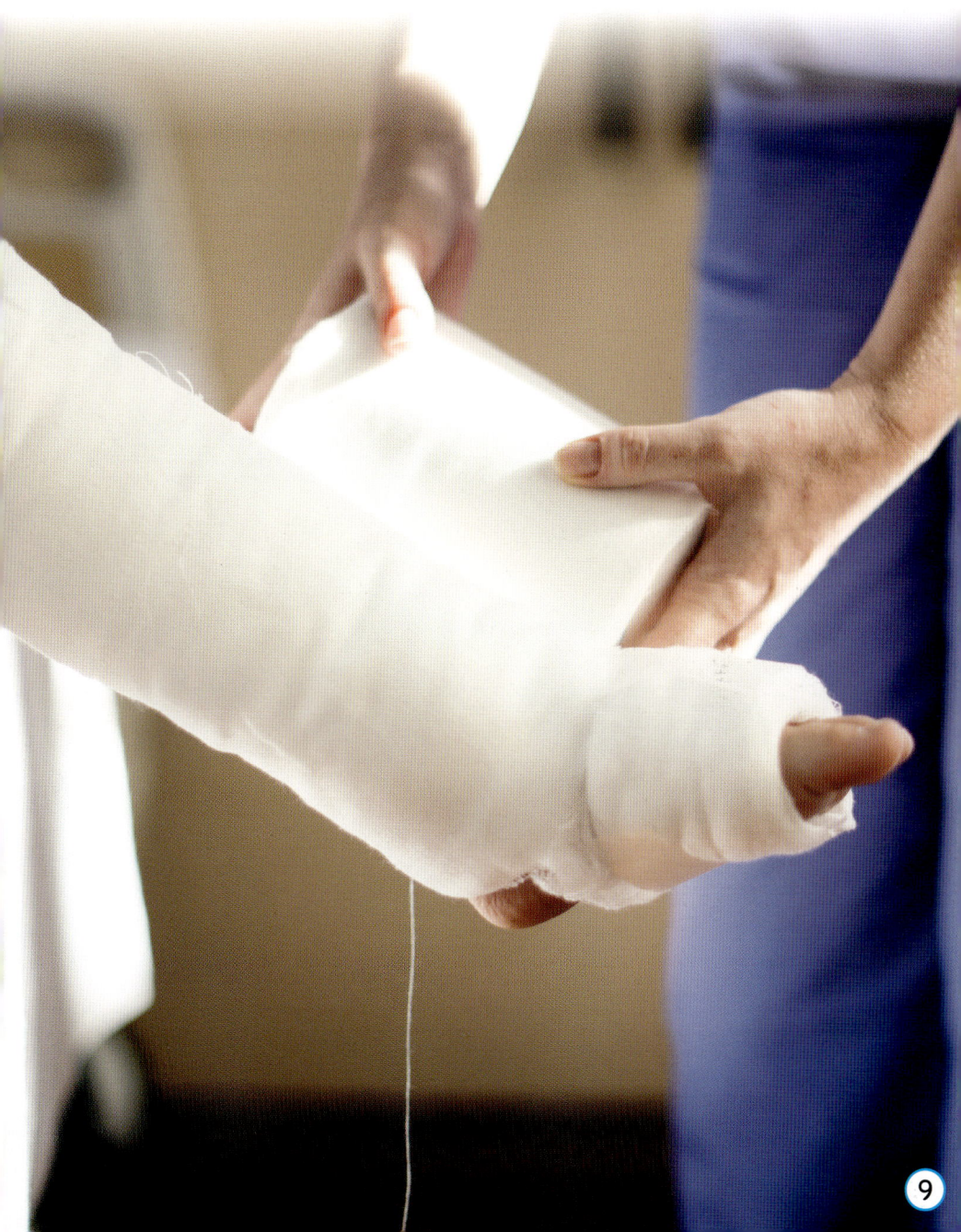

Now they can be sure that her leg will be kept still.

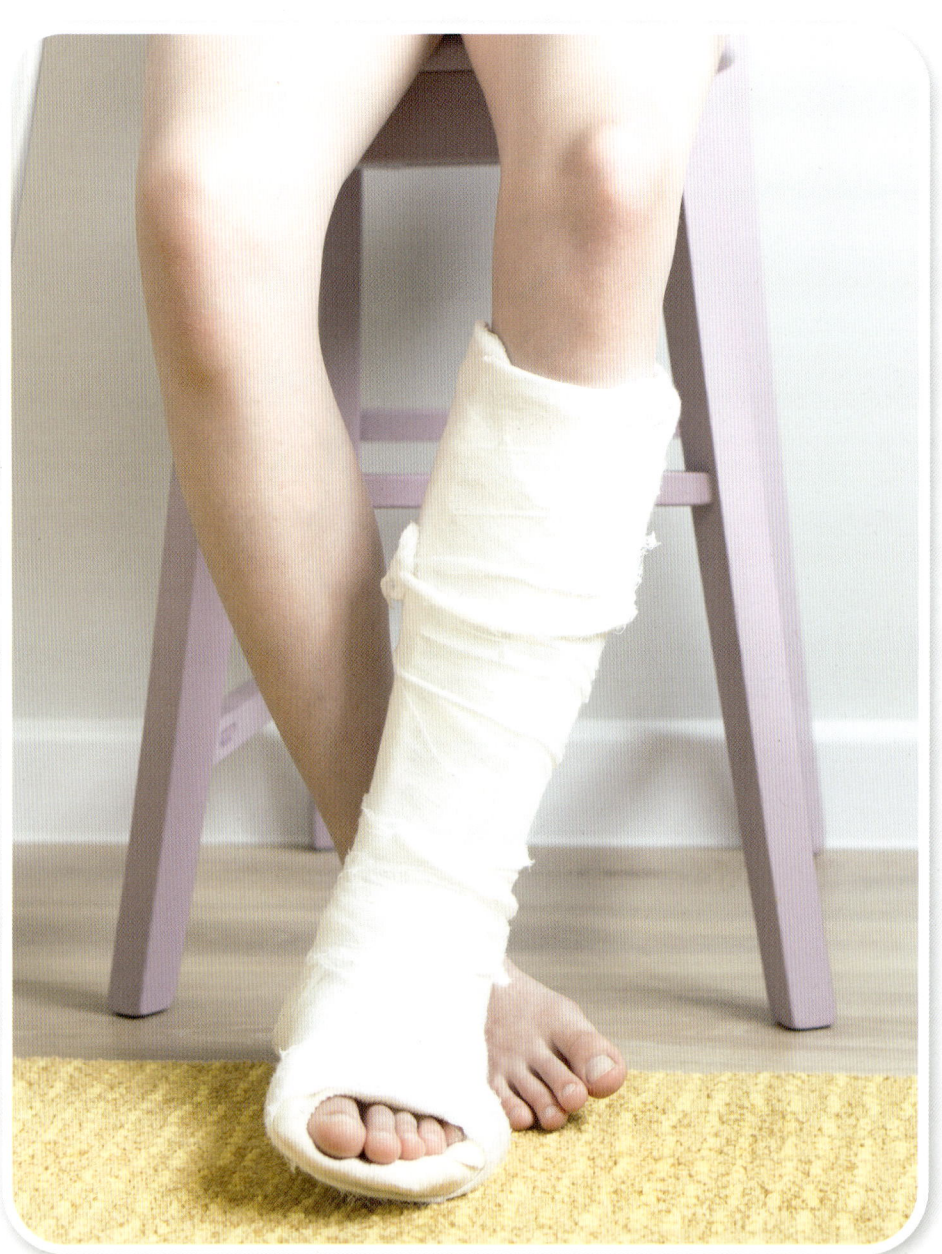

They will tell her how long the cast will need to be on her leg.

She must wait and allow the leg to rest. She must not run on it.

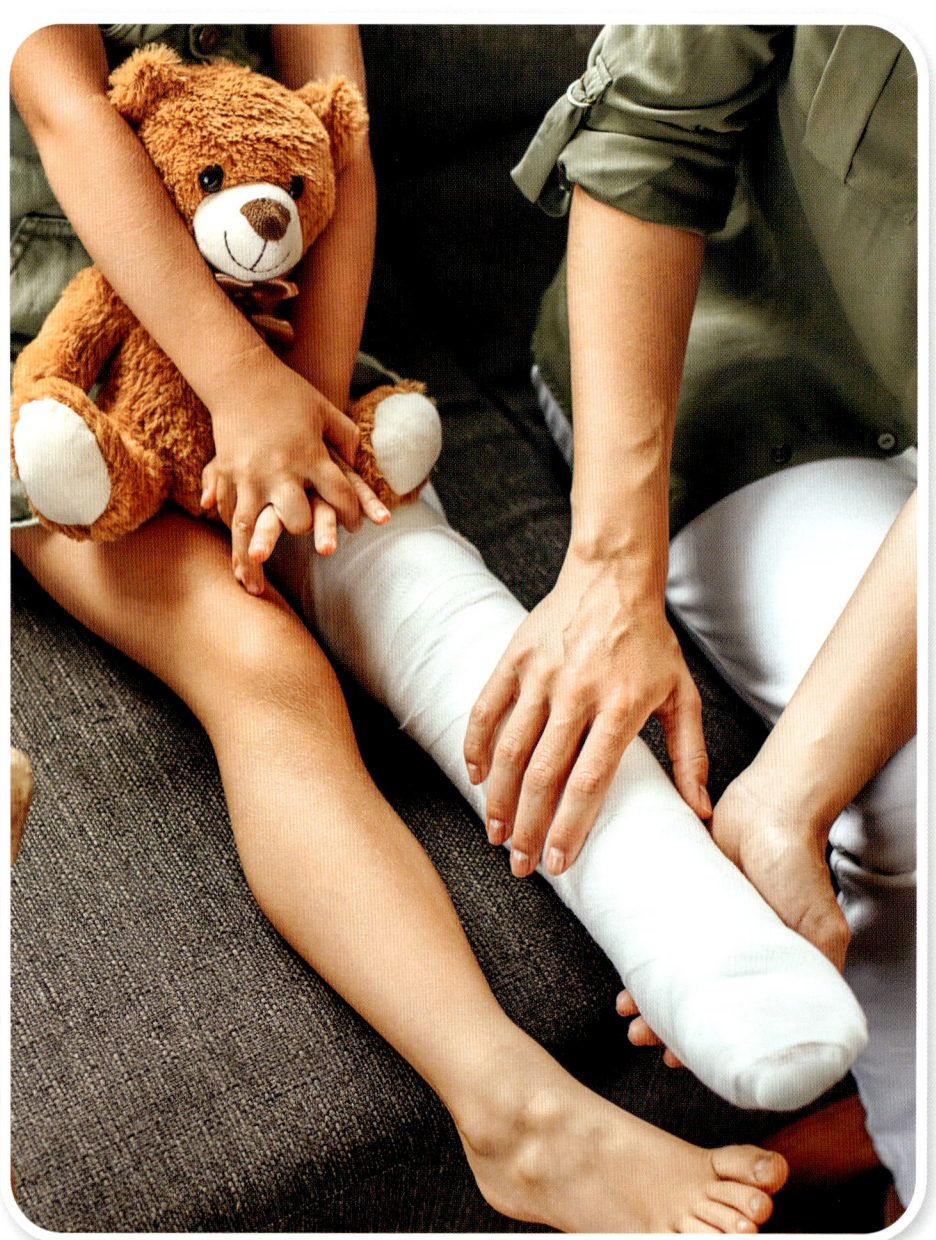

A cast can have pictures on it.
You can do it with felt pens.

Her cast will be cut off when the leg is better.

She can run with no pain now.
They did cure her leg!

©2023 BookLife Publishing Ltd.
King's Lynn, Norfolk, PE30 4LS, UK

ISBN 978-1-80505-049-0

All rights reserved. Printed in China.
A catalogue record for this book is
available from the British Library.

In a Cast
Written by Charis Mather
Designed by Jasmine Pointer

An Introduction to BookLife Readers...

Our Readers have been specifically created in line with the London Institute of Education's approach to book banding and are phonetically decodable and ordered to support each phase of Letters and Sounds.

Each book has been created to provide the best possible reading and learning experience. Our aim is to share our love of books with children, providing both emerging readers and prolific page-turners with beautiful books that are guaranteed to provoke interest and learning, regardless of ability.

BOOK BAND GRADED using the Institute of Education's approach to levelling.

PHONETICALLY DECODABLE supporting each phase of Letters and Sounds.

EXERCISES AND QUESTIONS to offer reinforcement and to ascertain comprehension.

CLEAR DESIGN to inspire and provoke engagement, providing the reader with clear visual representations of each non-fiction topic.

AUTHOR INSIGHT:
CHARIS MATHER

Charis Mather is a children's author at BookLife Publishing who has a love for reading and writing. Her studies in linguistics and experiences working with young readers have given her a knack for writing material that suits a range of ages and skill levels. Charis is passionate about producing books that emphasise the fun in reading and is convinced that no matter how much you already know, there is always something new to learn.

PHASE 4 /ow/ /ure/

This book focuses on /ow/ and /ure/ and is a Blue level 4 book band.

Image Credits Images are courtesy of Shutterstock.com. With thanks to Getty Images, Thinkstock Photo and iStockphoto. Cover – Lyakhova Evgeniya, sdecoret, Nadia Snopek. 4–5 – Kekyalyaynen, Monkey Business Images. 6–7 – Poznyakov, Sergey Ryzhov. 8–9 – Grzegorz Placzek, Rawpixel.com. 10–11 – Lyakhova Evgeniya, Yuganov Konstantin. 12–13 – ORION PRODUCTION. 14–15 – CandyBox Images, Kichigin.